Praise for Suddenly Stardust

"Don't let her humble and even occasionally timid way fool you. Joanne Brokaw is a powerhouse theatrical improvisor. Her reflections in this book are at once insightful and revealing. If you have any desire to expand your horizons as a performer, Joanne's stories can certainly prepare you for what and who you might encounter."

Law Tarello, MFA
Faculty, The Second City

"A fascinating memoir that recounts the transformation from beginner to capable improviser and the emotional growing pains that come with that metamorphosis. *Suddenly Stardust* is essential reading and earns its place on my bookshelf right between *Truth in Comedy* and the *UCB Manual*."

Austin Scott
House Improv Theater
Gainesville Florida

"Brokaw reminds us in *Suddenly Stardust* that time spent studying whatever it is we happen to love—be it yoga or ceramics or surfing—will likely reap a harvest of fruits we never knew we planted. Yes, improv teaches us to be looser, more creative performers. But much more importantly, it teaches us to listen, and give, and take, and color outside the lines."

Roberta Gore
Author of *Saving Grace*

"I was at first dismayed to see there were 142 pages, about improv for God's sake! But this book is not about improvising on stage. It's about improvising your way through life, complete with all doubts, fears, truths, failures, and successes. To anyone who is considering this—you will love this book."

Richard Hughson
Comedian, Storyteller

"I love this book, *Suddenly Stardust,* by Joanne Brokaw! It is a guide to life, showing how improv can act as a template for living fully with others. Improv can help us appreciate every single moment, be more creative, and remind us how stellar we are. Say 'Yes, I'll get this book.' And read it in one sitting, like I did. Then cherish it like I do."

Wendy Liebman
Comedian

"Finally, someone who gets it! Improv isn't about being funny. It's about letting go of fear in all aspects of communication and your life. Joanne Brokaw really gets it and conveys it!"

Scott Baker
from the comedy team Isaacs and Baker

"In *Suddenly Stardust*, Joanne Brokaw takes the reader backstage (and onstage) with her as she braves the challenging and terrifying world of improv. Her lessons learned will reverberate long with readers—and perhaps inspire them to say, 'Yes, and' to purposeful, compassionate living a little more often."

Carrie Anne Noble,
author of *The Mermaid's Sister* and *The Gold-Son*

SUDDENLY STARDUST

Suddenly Stardust
Copyright © 2019
Elizabeth Joanne Brokaw

Cover concept and design by Jonathan Grisham for Grisham Designs
Author photo by Jesse Sprinkle
Library of Congress Control Number:2019945194
ISBN: 978-1-948679-49-7

All rights reserved. No part of this book may be reproduced, stored in a retrieval system, or transmitted in any form or by any means—electronic, mechanical, photocopy, recording or otherwise—without the prior written permission of the publisher. The only exception is brief quotations for review purposes.

Published by WordCrafts Press
Cody, Wyoming 82414
www.wordcrafts.net

Suddenly Stardust

A MEMOIR (OF SORTS) ABOUT FEAR, FREEDOM & IMPROV

JOANNE BROKAW

WordCrafts

For Dave

"To him who is afraid, everything rustles."
Sophocles

"Try not giving a fuck. There's a lot of power in that."
"GLOW"

I sit in silence, staring at the blank screen.

The blank screen screams at me in response:

"You don't know how to write a book about improv!"

I wait a moment, eyes locked on this white empty square that is my partner on this creative journey. I wait a little more, feeling the pressure of the computer keys under my fingers, hearing the silence as it helps to form my thoughts, feeling my anxious heartbeat slow as it begins to sync with the energy that now envelops me.

I type:

"Yes, and... this is not a book about improv."

This is not a book about improv. This is not a book about the history of improv or improv theory or a biography of great improvisors or even a manual on how to play improv games or perform a Harold.

This is not a how-to manual to help you get over anxiety/depression/addiction to Pinterest/Netflix/refined sugar. This is not a book about how to write a book about improv or comedy or walking your dog.

This book is a simple little collection of things I've learned while doing improv, things that opened my eyes to the wonder and adventure I'd been missing for most of my life, thoughts I've passed on to friends as I convinced them to try an improv class, and some of the lessons I've learned that have made me a better human.

And we'll see that scene in three, two...

ONCE UPON A TIME
THERE WAS A GIRL WHO WAS ALWAYS AFRAID.

I was 50 years old when I took my first improv class. I'd wanted to do something fun and different to celebrate this maturity milestone, so I posted on Facebook and threw out the idea to my friends that we get together for a free improv workshop happening a few weeks after my actual birthday.

Dozens of people responded. "Sounds like fun!" they said. "I've always wanted to try that!" said a few others.

When it came time to actually go to the workshop, though, everyone bailed. Almost every excuse began with "I could never" or "I'm afraid".

If there was a land called I Could Never Because I'm Afraid, I would be the queen. I would sit on an enormous throne wearing a mighty crown and regal robes, and I'd be known far and wide for my ability to come up with excuses to avoid doing even the things I actually wanted to do.

But when the calendar marked my 50th year, I hopped a train from the land of I Could Never and got off at the next station, Maybe I Can.

All of my friends were afraid to try improv, even if it was to celebrate my half century of existence.

So I went to the improv workshop alone.

Once Upon a Time

Because, suddenly, I was afraid not to.

THE ONLY THING YOU HAVE TO FEAR
IS DOING IT WRONG

THINGS I FEARED ABOUT DOING IMPROV:
I would say something stupid.
I would do something stupid.
I would look stupid while simultaneously saying
                              and doing something stupid.
I would do it wrong.
I would offend someone.
Someone would offend me.
I wouldn't understand what was going on.
I would be so much older than the other people playing
        that I wouldn't understand any of their references.
I would do it wrong.
People would laugh at me behind my back.
People would not laugh at me on stage.
I would hate being on stage.
I would love being on stage but no one would let me be on stage.
I would do it wrong.
I would make my teammates look bad.
My teammates would abandon me
          in the middle of a scene, on stage, during a show.
I would wear the wrong clothes.
I would hurt myself.
I would hurt someone else.

I would do it wrong.

The Only Thing You Have to Fear

But if there's one thing I've learned in life it's that if you just follow the rules, everything will be OK. So when I started doing improv, I immediately took note of the rules—what you're supposed to do, and when, and how, things like:

Suddenly Stardust

Say yes to everything.
Never say no.
Don't ask questions.
Define your relationship as soon as possible.
Don't deny reality.
Show, don't tell.
Be specific.
Don't do teaching or transaction scenes.
Don't plan ahead.
Just make a bold move.
Don't make someone crazy or drunk in a scene.
Play at the top of your intelligence.
Pin your hair back so the audience can see your face.
Don't stand on stage with your hands in your pockets.

The Only Thing You Have to Fear

I like rules. I like order and structure. I like to know the logistics of the exercise I'm about to do so I know if I'm doing it right.

Because, god forbid, I do it wrong. I try, at all costs, to avoid doing anything wrong, and if I can't be sure I can do it right then I'll just avoid doing it at all.

Maybe you've heard of this affliction?

It's called paralysis by analysis.

The Only Thing You Have to Fear

I quickly became aware of the degree to which this over-analysis and desire to do the right thing squashed my ability to live in the moment. Because improv is all about responding only to the person standing in front of you—not thinking ahead to what they might say and how you'll respond. Every sentence back and forth is like peeling away the layers of the reality you're exploring together, moment by moment.

So you miss out on the adventure when you adhere too strictly to rules that say "Always do this" and "Never do that," because "doing this" or "saying that" can lead you to wild and wondrous places.

But it took me a long time to realize that, and it started with a handful of far more experienced improvisors who simply said:

The Only Thing You Have to Fear

"Fuck the rules."

This made me nervous. How would I know if I was doing it right without rules?

The Only Thing You Have to Fear

SCENE FROM AN IMPROV GAME

The game is Good Advice, Bad Advice. Three IMPROVISORS take the stage, in character, to give advice to an AUDIENCE MEMBER who has a question.

AUDIENCE MEMBER: What's the best way to take care of my dog?
IMPROVISOR 1: You should create a space with clear boundaries, like a big yard with a fence. That way your dog has room to explore but is safe from dangers.
IMPROVISOR 2: No. You should keep your dog on a very short leash at all times, even in the house.
IMPROVISOR 3: You should let your dog be a dog, man. Just open the door in the morning and let him run free all day.
IMPROVISOR 2: Your dog needs a leash. That way, it'll always be next to you, and you can control it, and you will always know where it is and what it's doing, and it can never do anything wrong.
IMPROVISOR 1: That seems cruel. The dog needs freedom to...
IMPROVISOR 2: A dog doesn't need freedom. A dog should obey. That's why you have a dog. So you have something to control.
IMPROVISOR 3: No! A dog needs to be free! No restrictions on wild animals. Run free, dogs, run free!

IMPROVISOR 1: Running loose can be dangerous. What if he gets hit by a car?

IMPROVISOR 3: If he gets hit by a car, then he gets hit by a car. That's just the circle of life.

IMPROVISOR 1: But shouldn't you care about safety while your dog explores new things?

IMPROVISOR 2: Everything new is dangerous.

IMPROVISOR 3: You can't explore anything if you're tied up with a leash.

IMPROVISOR 1: I think if you love your dog, you can give him clear boundaries so he can feel free to explore new things in a safe way.

IMPROVISOR 2: Freedom is dangerous. You need rules so no one makes decisions on their own.

IMPROVISOR 3: Fuck the rules.

The Only Thing You Have to Fear

SCENE FROM AN IMPROV WORKSHOP

INSTRUCTOR: We're going to do an exercise where we'll work on establishing the who, what, and where in a scene, but we're going to do it in just three sentences. The key is to tell us as much as you can about your relationship in those three sentences. Got it? Two people up!

Two women step on stage; the INSTRUCTOR gives them the suggestion "siblings."
The women turn to face each other.

IMPROVISOR 1: OK, Mary Jane, now that you, my sister, are here with me in the kitchen to bake the cookies for Mom's funeral, we can talk about the will.
IMPROVISOR 2: I'm sure Mom left both of us equal shares of everything.
IMPROVISOR 1: Even though I always do all of the work.

The two women shrug at each other and turn to the INSTRUCTOR.

INSTRUCTOR: OK, that was good. You followed the rules exactly. Let's try it again. But this time, step out and start performing an action, and let that breathe for a moment.

Then, instead of using words, see if you can use silence and actions to tell us what your relationship is and how you might be feeling about each other. So one person will say a sentence, but before the other person can respond, she needs to count to five. Willing to give it another try?

The two women nod. IMPROVISOR 1 steps to one side. She's mixing something in a bowl and scooping something onto a tray; her action is repetitive but she's moving with intent. Meanwhile IMPROVISOR 2 pulls a chair to centerstage, sits down, and starts flipping through the pages of a newspaper.

IMPROVISOR 2: (*sighs lazily*)
IMPROVISOR 1: (*sighs in return, a little more loudly, opening an oven and putting the tray inside*)

IMPROVISOR 2 looks up from her paper; IMPROVISOR 1 glances over her shoulder at IMPROVISOR 2 and scowls. IMPROVISOR 2 shrugs. Three, two, one...

IMPROVISOR 1: I'm nervous about the reading of Mom's will today.

The silence hangs heavy in the air as IMPROVISOR 2 turns another page of the newspaper, leans back in the chair and stretches her arms, yawns. Three, two, one...

IMPROVISOR 2: Why? I'm sure Mom was as fair in death as she was in life.
The silence is now charged with tension as IMPROVISOR 1 shakes her head and stirs and scoops with more force. She is taking

deep breaths and exhaling loudly. When she responds, her words are clipped, and succinct. Three, two, one...

IMPROVISOR 1: Well, then *you* clearly have nothing to worry about.
INSTRUCTOR: Scene!

The two women go to center stage; they're smiling and nodding at each other.

INSTRUCTOR: Do you see the difference? Both times, you followed the rules. But the first time around, you just gave us information, while the second time around, you gave us a reality, emotion, backstory, and so much more to work with.

Both women are nodding. They have just unwittingly learned a lesson in listening and responding honestly, the importance of letting silence settle in a scene, and what it means to show and not tell.

Oh, and how following the rules can be much more nuanced than either of them imagined.

Over time, I've learned the dos, don'ts, and rules of improv can be boiled down to these guidelines:

The Only Thing You Have to Fear

Accept and heighten whatever my scene partner
is giving me, because my scene partner is the
most important person on stage, and it's
my job to make her look good, so I
should always listen and respond
honestly because there are
no mistakes in improv,
only happy accidents.

YES, AND

One of the most common mistakes improvisors make, especially new improvisors, is to think that they have to come to a scene with something they're going to initiate and then convince their scene partner to go along with.

"Well, I planned for that scene to be about two kids on a playground," an improvisor might say, irritated, because he initiated the scene as a character who was clearly a child, skipping onto the stage and singing "The Alphabet Song." Except his scene partner came out hunched over like an old woman pushing a walker. The first improvisor spoke in his childlike voice; the second improvisor responded in the slow, gravely voice.

The first improvisor was at a total loss, because his plan had been ruined.

So rather than ditch his own idea and see where this new scenario might go, he insisted his scene partner was a child pretending to be an old woman, leaving her to justify this change. And what could have been a fascinating scene about an old woman and a child on a playground was shoehorned into a box by one improvisor unwilling to give up on his idea.

It doesn't mean the scene was bad. It may even have been good. The audience may even have laughed.

But the first improvisor missed the opportunity to see what would have happened if he had just let the magic take his hand and lead him into the unknown.

Yes, And

This is why most beginner improv classes start by teaching the fundamental rule of improv: Yes, And.

Yes, And, which is sometimes described as Accept and Heighten, is one of the foundational ways you can support your scene partner. One exercise new improvisors do to practice this skill goes like this:

IMPROVISOR 1: I'm going to yoga this afternoon.
IMPROVISOR 2: YES, you're going to yoga this afternoon, AND after that we'll have lunch.
IMPROVISOR 1: YES, after that we'll have lunch, AND then we'll talk about that lipstick on your collar.
IMPROVISOR 2: YES, we'll talk about that lipstick on my collar, AND then I'll call my lawyer.

Unfortunately, Yes, And is sometimes taught as Never Say No, and that's really not the same thing. Saying Yes, And in improv means that the *improvisors* always agree to the reality they're exploring, but the *characters* are free to say no, if that's what they naturally would do. For example:

IMPROVISOR 1: Hey, Joe! I got us tickets to ride the roller coaster at Seabreeze!
IMPROVISOR 2: No way, Sam. You know I hate roller coasters.
IMPROVISOR 1: I know, but it's a wooden roller coaster. It's not as fast as the newer ones.
IMPROVISOR 2: You're always trying to get me to do things you know I hate.

If saying no is what Joe would normally do (and if I was Joe my answer would definitely have been a big, fat no), then it's OK to explore that. But what if...

Yes, And

...after initially saying no Joe finally said yes and got on a roller coaster? And hated it? And threw up and cried and made a spectacle of himself in public? Or even better...

...loved it and wanted to start trying all sorts of new things, getting crazier and crazier and crazier, until the roles reversed and now *Sam* started balking at *Joe's* ideas? Wouldn't *that* be fun to watch?

Yes, And

Oh, the possibilities when we just say yes.

SCENE FROM A MARRIAGE

He stands in the kitchen, describing in detail the plan he has to build a garden in the back yard. It involves 4x4 lumber and regrading the lawn and power tools and truckloads of dirt.

She does not want a garden in the back yard. Not now, at least. He has talked for years about building a huge boxed garden in this spot because, then, she had wanted a garden. She once even purchased blueberry bushes to have him plant in the garden he promised to create. But he never planted some of the bushes, and the ones he did plant she could never get to thrive. He did not want blueberry bushes; she does not want this garden anymore.

This promises to be a stressful discussion.

But lately she is trying to apply to her daily life some of what she's learned in improv, and she decides that, as an experiment, she will Yes, And this idea—even if he isn't Yes, Anding back—and see what happens.

HIM: ...and I'm guessing that if I dig down about six to eight inches and then build the retaining wall about two feet high, that should be sturdy enough.

HER: Yes, that should be sturdy enough. And you can put whatever plants you'd like in there.

HIM: Well, this is your garden. I'm building this for you. What would you like me to plant there?

HER: Um, yes, you're building it for me. You could plant blueberry bushes.
HIM: No, we tried blueberry bushes. They never grew. No, we're not planting blueberry bushes.

She can think of several reasons why the blueberries never grew, and is ready to begin arguing about that. Instead, she replies...

Her: Yes, we were not able to grow blueberries in that spot. We should plant something that will grow there without too much work.
Him: That's a great idea. You're in charge of the plants. I'm going to get some lumber.

And so he begins the garden project. For the next two weeks, every day after work he cuts and saws and hammers and digs in the dirt. Normally, she would be outside with him, giving her thoughts and opinions about the project, worried that he was ruining the lawn, stressed about how much work this new garden will be, or how much money they were spending on something they don't need and she doesn't even want.

Instead, she Yes, Ands everything he says. She doesn't offer advice or opinions; in fact, other than to come outside once a while to let the dogs out and say, "It looks great!", she stays away from the project site and lets him work in peace.

And then one day, the garden is done. She has to admit that it's a lovely garden. The retaining wall is solid and garden space is roomy, and he's taken great care to prepare the soil for whatever plants will call it home. And while it takes up a large portion of the back yard, she can finally see why he thought this was a good idea.

HIM: It's your garden. We could put blueberries in here if you still want to.
HER: Yes, we could plant blueberries. But I think you should pick out plants that you really like.
HIM: Well, I've been thinking…

And he talks at length about the research he's been doing and the plants he's considering and the colors he's chosen, and together they go to the garden store, where they both agree that a butterfly bush should be the centerpiece of the garden. And they haul home a carload of other plants, too, and he puts them all in the ground.

And when he's done they stand together, admiring his weeks of hard work.

HIM: Well, it's finished. It looks great!
HER: Yes, it looks great! And thank you.

Yes, And

This is one reason why sometimes improv feels like therapy, only more intense and less expensive.

As I've grown in my improv experience, the concept of strictly adhering to Yes, And has morphed into a better understanding that Yes, And really means:

Yes, And

Assume everything your partner says or gives to you is a gift
                              meant for your benefit.
Accept that gift graciously, even if it's not
        what you expected to receive.
Add something of yourself to it,
something true and honest.
Return it to them.
Repeat.

This is a good recipe for improv...

Yes, And

...and life.

QUESTION TIME

SCENE FROM A WORKSHOP: PART 1

INSTRUCTOR is speaking to a group of IMPROVISORS with varying degrees of experience.

INSTRUCTOR: We're going to play a game. Everyone on stage.

The IMPROVISORS get on stage.

INSTRUCTOR: Make two lines. Two people to the center. We'll do some scenes, but you can only ask each other questions.
IMPROVISOR 1: Any kind of questions?
INSTRUCTOR: Yes, just keep asking questions.
IMPROVISOR 1: That's it? There aren't any other rules?
INSTRUCTOR: Stop asking questions about the rules. Just go with it and we'll talk about it when it's over. And we'll see that scene...
IMPROVISOR 2: Are you going to be home tonight?
IMPROVISOR 1: Why?

INSTRUCTOR stops the scene
INSTRUCTOR: No, no. Don't ask "why". You want to ask questions that keep the scene going.

Question Time

IMPROVISOR 1: Oh, I'm sorry. I didn't understand.
INSTRUCTOR: Try again.
IMPROVISOR 2: Did you finish the project?
IMPROVISOR 1: When did you need it by?
IMPROVISOR 2: Why?
IMPROVISOR 1 *(turns to instructor)*: Wait. I thought we weren't supposed to ask why?
INSTRUCTOR: That one was fine. Just keep going. Keep asking questions.
IMPROVISOR 1: I'm confused.
INSTRUCTOR: Just keep asking questions.

The scene ends quickly as IMPROVISOR 2 can't think of a question. Everyone laughs. IMPROVISOR 3 takes IMPROVISOR 2's place. IMPROVISOR 1 continues asking questions, concentrating on not making a mistake. IMPROVISOR 3 soon falters; everyone laughs. IMPROVISORS 4, 5, and 6 rotate through.

Finally INSTRUCTOR calls the end of the game. IMPROVISOR 1 is feeling confident; she has wrangled the game and won.

INSTRUCTOR *(to group)*: So was that a fun game to watch?

IMPROVISORS shrug. INSTRUCTOR looks at IMPROVISOR 1, standing alone in the center of the stage.

INSTRUCTOR: The point of the game is not to be the last person standing.
IMPROVISOR 1 *(feeling uncomfortable)*: I didn't know that.
INSTRUCTOR: It's not a contest.
IMPROVISOR 1: I'm sorry. I'm confused. You said to keep asking questions.

INSTRUCTOR: The point of the game is to make mistakes. It's funny. The point is not to keep asking questions until you're the last person standing.

IMPROVISOR 1 (*embarrassed, tears welling up in her eyes*): I wish you had told me that before we started.

INSTRUCTOR: I assumed you'd figure it out as we went along.

IMPROVISOR 1: Clearly I didn't.

IMPROVISOR 1 leaves the stage in tears.

Question Time

THINGS IMPROV TEACHERS HAVE TOLD ME:

You ask too many questions.
You're in your head too much.
You worry too much about rules.

None of that feedback is helpful.

SCENE FROM A WORKSHOP: PART 2

INSTRUCTOR, to a group of IMPROVISORS with varying degrees of experience.

INSTRUCTOR: We're going to do an exercise called Questions. Two by two you're going to do a scene, but you can only speak to each other in questions. Take your time, and try to ask questions that keep the scene going. If you don't ask a question or you repeat a question you're out, and someone will take your place. Make sense?

IMPROVISORS look at each other; a few nod, a few shrug.

INSTRUCTOR: The point of the exercise is not to be the last person standing. The point is to show how hard it is to perform a good scene when you're only asking questions. Feel free to screw up, give up, and please, have fun. There are no wrong answers. Does that make sense?

IMPROVISORS nod.

INSTRUCTOR: Let's try it!

IMPROVISORS perform two person scenes, asking questions,

Question Time

failing to ask questions, laughing. This goes on for some time, as everyone is clearly having fun.

INSTRUCTOR: Scene! How did that feel?
IMPROVISOR 2: That was hard to keep up.
IMPROVISOR 3: I ran out of things to ask.
IMPROVISOR 4: Some questions were OK. But after a while, we weren't really saying anything.
IMPROVISOR 5: It was hard to Yes, And.

IMPROVISOR 1 says nothing.

INSTRUCTOR: Great feedback! Asking questions can be fine, if what you're asking helps to move the scene along. But if all you do is ask questions like "What are you doing" or "Why are you doing that" or "What is this", then you're making your scene partner do all the work.

IMPROVISORS are nodding.

INSTRUCTOR: And we talked about how being a good scene partner means gifting your partner with something they can add to and gift back to you.

IMPROVISORS nod enthusiastically.

INSTRUCTOR: Hopefully that makes sense. Anyone have questions?

IMPROVISOR 1 does not raise her hand. She does not have any questions. She does not cry. This is a safe place.

SORRY, NOT SORRY

THINGS I HAVE APOLOGIZED FOR DURING OR AFTER AN IMPROV PRACTICE OR SHOW:

Being in the way.
Taking the lead.
Not taking the lead.
Interrupting.
Freezing in the middle of a scene.
Being bossy.
Sweeping a scene too early.
Having to take a potty break in the middle of practice.
Talking too much.
Asking too many questions.
Asking more questions to clarify the questions
    I've already asked because the answers were too vague.
Answering other people's questions,
              especially ones no one has asked (yet).
Making a bad choice.
Having fun.
Crying.
Apologizing.

This is a perfect example of art imitating life.

Sorry, Not Sorry

SCENE IN A GROCERY STORE, PART 1:

WOMAN 1 is pushing a cart through the produce aisle, turns a corner and meets WOMAN 2 head on. There is no collision; they are simply both in the same small space.

WOMAN 1: I'm sorry.
WOMAN 2: I'm sorry.

They both back up and indicate to the other to go through the space first.

WOMAN 1: I'm sorry. You go first.
WOMAN 2: I'm sorry. No, you, please.
WOMAN 1: Haha, I'm sorry, it's OK. I'm going to …
WOMAN 2: Haha, I'm sorry, I was headed…

WOMAN 1 and WOMAN 2 continue smiling as they each back up and go down different aisles.

SCENE IN A GROCERY STORE, PART 2:

WOMAN 1 is pushing a cart through the dairy aisle, encounters a roadblock. WOMAN 3 has parked her cart on one side of the aisle but is standing on the other side of the aisle with the dairy cooler door open. The cart is slightly askew. The aisle is blocked; no one can pass.

WOMAN 1 *(after waiting for a few moments)*: I'm sorry, excuse me, would you mind if I squeezed by?
WOMAN 3 *(quickly closes the dairy door and scurries to move her cart)*: Oh, I'm so sorry about that.
WOMAN 1: I'm sorry. Thank you.
WOMAN 3: I'm sorry

WOMAN 3 smiles. WOMAN 1 smiles.

WOMAN 1: Sorry.

Sorry, Not Sorry

SCENE IN A GROCERY STORE, PART 3:

WOMAN 1 is standing in the cereal aisle. One side of the aisle is blocked by a display of granola bars. MAN is pushing his cart down the aisle. When he encounters the crowded aisle, he swerves directly towards WOMAN 1, who moves quickly to avoid being hit. She stumbles, knocking down the display of granola bars in the process.

WOMAN 1: I'm sorry.
MAN: No problem.

MAN reaches over WOMAN 1 and the pile of granola bars, grabs a box of cereal, and then pushes his cart away to continue shopping. WOMAN kneels down to pick up the granola bars and reassemble the display.

THINGS YOU PROBABLY SHOULD APOLOGIZE FOR IN IMPROV:

Pushing someone off the stage.

THIS FUCKING GUY

Suddenly Stardust

I'm standing in my back yard, the sun just barely peeking over the neighbor's garage roof. The dog is sniffing around along the fence, tracking the stray cats, raccoons, and opossum that pass through our yard in the night time.

Other than the sound of the dog snuffing as he sucks up scents, the only thing I can hear is birdsong.

There is soft tweeting and chirping in the bushes, and the leaves rustle as my winged friends shake off their dreams. I open the large storage can where I keep the birdseed and prepare to lay out the buffet.

That's when nature kicks into high gear.

The sparrows call to the sparrows. The chickadees call to the chickadees. The blue jay calls to his mate. The juncos and tufted titmouses and mourning doves and nuthatches and crows call to their own in their secret song, "It's time for breakfast! Pass it on!"

Different birds performing their differing morning ablutions, who then shift gears in unison for the same group activity, flocking to the feeder where they jostle and flutter, the chickadees and sparrows tossing seeds from the feeder to the ground, where the juncos are waiting. When the blue jay announces his arrival with a screech, all part to let him have the pick of the seeds, and then as one they return to breakfast.

This happens every morning, in almost exactly the

This Fucking Guy

same manner. I open the birdseed can, the birds make the announcement, everyone eats.

There are no reservations taken for a spot at the bird feeder, no plan made the night before about who will eat and when and how. Despite their differing dialects and wants and needs, the birds think and act in unison.

As I stand there in the morning chill, I hear a loud, intermittent drumming above my head, completely out of sync with the rest of the morning activity.

It's the woodpecker, drilling in the gigantic sugar maple. Even if I don't see him he leaves his mark on the garage eaves; branches, riddled with his work, fall to the ground whenever the wind blows.

Right now, he's seeking out his own breakfast, in his own time, and on his own terms, regardless of how his independent activity disrupts the perfect flow of everyone else.

Damned woodpecker. Always disrupting the group mind.

SCENE FROM AN IMPROV PRACTICE

COACH: Let's do some three line scenes. Each person says one line at a time, three lines, then we switch. Got it? Two people up.

IMPROVISOR 1: I'm never going to lose these last 10 pounds before the wedding.

IMPROVISOR 2: Good thing your dress has that giant bow on the back.

IMPROVISOR 1: Thanks for always looking on the bright side.

COACH: Great. Make sense? Two more people. Three lines, one line at a time.

IMPROVISOR 3: I'm glad you could meet me for coffee.

IMPROVISOR 4: This is the worst coffee in the world. Why do we always have to meet at this shitty coffee shop?

IMPROVISOR 3: It's close to the office.

COACH: Great! Next...

IMPROVISOR 4: I can't have coffee. Interferes with my Viagra. You know that! Last night? Heh heh heh.

IMPROVISOR 3: Um...

COACH: Um...

IMPROVISOR 4: Hey, have I shown you my gun? It's a Glock 9 mm. Here, you wanna hold it?

IMPROVISOR 3: *(silence)*

IMPROVISOR 4: It's rock hard. Unlike my dick, which is limp from all of this coffee. HAHAHA!
COACH: All right. Can we have two more people up? Please?
IMPROVISOR 4: Up! Unlike my dick!

So there's this guy. Let's call him Bobby.

Bobby is a stand up comic who started taking improv classes so he could, as he explained, learn how to be funnier.

Despite weeks and months of classes and play time, Bobby is still having trouble with the concept of Yes, And.

And teamwork.

Bobby will come into a scene, apropos of nothing, strutting across the stage to drop a random one-liner directly at the audience, and then walk out of the scene, leaving his teammates to justify who he was and why he was there and what he said and why he's now gone.

Bobby likes jokes about blow jobs and guns and knives. In any scene, you can be sure someone will be killed or kidnapped, usually as the result of a long-winded plot that ends with sex.

The irony is that off stage, Bobby is a pretty nice guy. Sure, he still likes crude jokes and monopolizing conversations, but if you needed it he would give you the shirt off his back and a $20 bill, too. He's maybe not the guy you want to invite to family dinner with your grandmother, but he's not an ogre.

But onstage?

Bobby is not funny.

In fact, on stage Bobby is a giant pain in the ass.

And now you find yourself on a team with Bobby for the next twelve weeks.

This Fucking Guy

Your first instinct is to sit this team session out to avoid having to deal with Bobby. You've been down this road before, with Bobby or other improvisors who are equally challenging to play with. So when you see Bobby walk in for the first practice, when your heart drops and the improv delight you have been anticipating goes up in smoke, you turn to a friend (who is a far more experienced improvisor than you are) to commiserate and hear your friend mutter, "Shit. Bobby."

You both grimace as you proceed with practice.

Afterward, you and your friend walk to your cars, and you're literally tearing up at the realization that both choices ahead of you—stop doing improv for this session or play with Bobby for twelve weeks—break your heart.

Your friend says, "Yeah, this sucks." Then he stops and turns to look you in the eye. "But it looks like we're both going to learn something about ourselves over the next few months."

THINGS YOU CAN DO WHEN YOU END UP PLAYING WITH BOBBY:

Stop whining.
Focus on your team's group mind.
Decide that you will do your best to make your scene partner look good, even if your scene partner is Bobby.
Yes, And the hell out of everything Bobby says.
Cringe at the words that come out of your mouth.
Stop worrying about how you look or sound.
Worry about being a good scene partner.
Let go of your own ideas about how the scene should go.
Stop worrying about whether or not the scene was good.
Listen to your coach and follow his suggestions.
Focus on being honest, not funny (or bitter).
Trust the rest of your team to have your back (and Bobby's, too).
Realize playing with Bobby is difficult, but not impossible.
Create bizarre characters in weird situations doing and saying things onstage you would never even contemplate offstage, because it's your job to justify whatever Bobby says or does.
Push yourself beyond your comfort zone.
Learn something about yourself.
Grow as an improvisor.

This Fucking Guy

Forget being the funniest person in the room. Get over the notion that the audience needs to remember your name. Whatever you're doing should support your scene partners and make them look good because, in improv...

Suddenly Stardust

Everyone is looking out for everyone else.
No one is alone.
It's mutually assured success.
But if you crash, you go down together.

This Fucking Guy

But if you're only trying to make the audience laugh, if you're so busy thinking of jokes that you're not listening to what's happening on stage, if you're trying to show what a great improvisor you are by showing what a shitty improvisor your scene partner is, then in improv, and probably in life...

...you're a jackass.

DEEP BREATHS AND STARDUST
AN INTERLUDE

Wherever you are, right now, take a moment to sit still and let your mind clear.

Breathe in, breathe out.

Feel the air as it enters your body, and then as it exits.

Take a moment to feel your heart beating in your chest, the blood flowing through your veins.

Feel the air around you as it touches your body. Maybe you're in a crowd right now and you feel someone's breath on the back of your neck. Maybe you're in a park and the breeze is lifting a strand of your hair. Maybe you're alone and you suddenly become aware of the stillness of space pressing against you, waking the tiny hairs on your arms and compressing your clothing even closer to your skin.

Take a moment to listen to the sounds around you. Maybe there's a dog snoring softly at your feet or the noise of traffic seeping in through a closed window. Maybe you hear waves crashing or people shouting or birdsong cascading from tree branches.

Maybe you think you hear nothing. Even in a sensory deprivation tank you will hear the sound of your own breathing. Silence is filled with sound, if we only take the time to listen.

Take a moment to smell the space around you, filled with the scent of flowers, exhaust fumes, cologne, scented candles, shampoo, laundry detergent. Perhaps the odor of lunch on the breath of the person next to you tickles your nostrils.

Deep Breaths and Stardust

Breathe in, breathe out.

Realize that space has a feel, a sound, a smell. Take a moment to acknowledge that you are part of that space, and that you bring to it your own experiences of the day, that the space you inhabit physically touches against others, that your existence has both a literal and figurative presence, has a sound that joins in the cacophony of life and a scent that perfumes the atmosphere.

Breathe in again, and this time imagine the air as it travels through your nostrils and down your windpipe and into your lungs, and imagine the oxygen escaping from that breath and entering into your bloodstream.

Exhale.

Researchers have looked for and found bits of space dust in the grime of urban areas, cosmic particles from the birth of our solar system, tiny bits from asteroids and meteors that exploded millions of light years away and then settled right here, under our noses.

They discovered that every day we not only touch these bits of exploded stars, but we inhale them with every breath.

Breathe deeply.

Feel this stardust as it leeches into your bloodstream, as your veins carry this extraterrestrial detritus throughout your body, as you physically become one with the heavens.

Breathe out and feel your lungs expel tiny molecules of your being along with air, small bits of your emotions and thoughts, tiny memories of your experiences and hopes and dreams that now leave your body through your lips and float away from you.

Imagine now a cloud hanging overhead filled with the thoughts and emotions and bits of other people around the world who are breathing along with you, the breath of your ancestors and their ancestors still lingering, mingling with space particles and stardust and molecules of human experience.

Breathe this in. Breathe it out.

There is no need to invent anything in improv. You are always surrounded by stories and experiences that have been happening for millennia and will continue long, long after you are gone.

You and your story are part of this cloud.

And it's all right there, this entire chronicle of human existence —our entire solar system and beyond—stretching forever behind you into the past and onwards to infinity, all before you on the stage, just waiting for you to call to it the moment you leave the sidelines with a movement, a line of dialogue, or simply one small step towards centerstage.

Waiting for you to simply make a bold move.

Deep Breaths and Stardust

You are born of the heavens, and whatever you bring to the stage will be beautiful, if you only let the stardust fall unhindered from your lips.

SOUNDS OF SILENCE

When I was in college, I had a film teacher who said, "The meaning of the film is found not on the image on the screen, but in the darkness between the frames."

This professor dropped so many deep comments into every lecture that a friend and I started keeping a notebook just to record his quirky thoughts and profound one-liners.

Thirty years later, I've lost the notebook and I've forgotten the other quotes, along with most of what I was supposed to learn in the class. But after all these years, that one quote has stuck with me.

Because he had gone on to explain his statement this way:

Our eyes actually see the image on the screen. Then, in that fraction of a fraction of a fraction of dark space between the cells of the film, a darkness we don't even realize is there, our brain actually processes what we just saw.

And gives it meaning.

Sounds of Silence

Dutch researchers studying silence and social needs found that when conversation is flowing easily between people, the people feel positive emotions and experience a "heightened sense of belonging, self-esteem, social validation, and consensus."

But when the conversation is disrupted by a silence of as little as four seconds, people begin to experience negative emotions, and even have feelings of rejection akin to ostracism.

It's probably the reason why new improvisors talk over each other in scenes. Part of it is the desire to get their idea out there. But it's also the belief that you have to say something, anything, because silence on stage is proof that you don't know what you're doing.

The reality, though, is that listening is one of the most important gifts you can give to your scene partner. Unfortunately, it's also one of the most difficult skills to hone.

Because in order to listen, you need the silence.

An improv instructor once had us do an exercise where two improvisors got on stage and didn't speak for 30 seconds. During the silence, they had to engage in some sort of activity—stirring a drink, rocking a baby, digging a hole, packing a suitcase.

Whoever eventually spoke first had to begin with the phrase "I love you." And it needed to be charged with emotion, any emotion —happiness, sadness, jealousy, anger, fear. (You get the picture.)

"I love you" seems like a pretty straightforward phrase. But if you know the words are coming while the emotion behind it is a mystery, it's not quite as easy to be prepared. In fact, if you're not paying attention to your scene partner, you could be blindsided. "I love you" said by someone who has been angrily packing a suitcase means something completely different than "I love you" spoken by someone coyishly batting their eyelashes, and they're both different from an "I love you" spoken by someone standing on a chair and waving as if from the window of a train.

And that was the point of the exercise. In improv, you have to be in the moment, responding honestly to *everything* that is happening between you and your scene partner, verbal and nonverbal.

The lesson? You can say more with fewer words
if you understand that silence has a voice.

GOT TO BE REAL

SCENE FROM AN IMPROV WORKSHOP:

Two IMPROVISORS are standing close together, in an area marked out to represent the space of an elevator. One pushes the floor button, and the two stand quietly for a moment.

IMPROVISOR 1 *(turns to IMPROVISOR 2, uses his forefinger and thumb to mimic a gun, points it at IMPROVISOR 2, almost making contact with his chest, and pulls the trigger):* Bang.
IMPROVISOR 2: You missed.

Got to be Real

We're about a dozen people in total, seated around heavy, iron patio tables with billowing maroon umbrellas, a small contingent of the conferees from the St. Davids Writers' Conference out for a creative nature walk on the hour and a half break between lunch and the afternoon sessions.

It's a gorgeous day, the sun high and bright in the sky, the birds, bunnies, and other critters active across the quad as we sit in quiet contemplation, pondering the writing prompt we've been given.

Roberta is not only the leader on this creative walk, she's my friend and roommate for the four days I'm at the conference. Our other roommate, Carrie, is the third part of a spectacular friendship triangle. They are the main reason I am here.

The writing prompts Roberta has chosen for this walk are taken from a Bible verse, Psalm 81:10, and are meant to explore what it means to, as she explains, "sow seeds for the Kingdom." She's going to have us focus on four things this afternoon: mercy, truth, righteousness, and peace.

This is what you'd expect at a conference on a Christian campus. Most of the people who are here write in the religious and inspirational genres—Christian fiction, non-fiction books about spiritual life, devotions and devotionals (and yes, there is a difference), poetry that glorifies God.

Me? I'm here to contemplate whatever messages the

universe, the muses, God, and that rabbit scurrying across the quad might have to offer.

Oh, and to finish writing the book you're holding in your hand.

But back to the prompt for this station on the walk. Right now, we're supposed to be pondering, and then writing about, truth.

"To write truth," Roberta says, "we first need to face truth."

She sets her timer for 10 minutes, and I start writing:

Got to be Real

If in order to write or speak the truth we first need to face it, it means we need to be walking through life with our eyes wide open to the reality in front of us.

The future isn't truth, because it hasn't happened yet. Even if the path you're on appears destined for some certain point ahead, it's all subject to the flap of a butterfly's wing in Africa, which could change the course of events in a millisecond and send you off into a hurricane.

The past isn't truth, not really, because it doesn't exist anymore, except in our memory. And we all have the ability to select that which we want to remember and then color it with whatever broad brush strokes we need in order to live with it, forget it, or hold on to it as either comfort or weapon.

Truth, then, is what is right in front of our noses. It's the ground beneath our feet, the air that we've inhaled and that sits in our lungs for a fraction of a heartbeat before being released on our next exhale.

To face the truth, to respond to and in the truth, means being present in this moment, with this person, in this reality.

In improv, as in life, this can be a difficult thing.

Got to be Real

SCENE FROM AN IMPROV WORKSHOP:

Two IMPROVISORS are on stage to do a scene. They're given the suggestion "coffee shop."

IMPROVISOR 1: *(speaking with an Irish accent)* Hey, Jack! It's good to see you again!
IMPROVISOR 2: *(nods solemnly)* I'll have a cappuccino.
IMPROVISOR 1: *(mimics making coffee, makes sounds of whirring and whooshing of machines)* So I saw that movie you were talking about yesterday. I agree. Totally under-appreciated. *(Hands coffee to IMPROVISOR 2.)*
IMPROVISOR 2: I don't know what you're talking about. We're in ancient Rome.
INSTRUCTOR: OK, stop for a second. Where did you both think this scene was taking place?
IMPROVISOR 1: A coffee shop?
INSTRUCTOR: In Ireland?
IMPROVISOR 1: Well, it could be Ireland. Or not. I mean, I just wanted to work on my Irish accent, and, like, Irish people are everywhere.
IMPROVISOR 2: They were not in ancient Rome.
INSTRUCTOR *(to IMPROVISOR 2)*: Why did you think this was ancient Rome?
IMPROVISOR 2: Because I had an idea to do a scene about

what it would be like to have a coffee shop in ancient Rome.
INSTRUCTOR: That's a great idea. But when the scene started, it seemed pretty clear that it wasn't ancient Rome. One of you had an Irish accent, and there was the sound of what were probably electric machines, right?
IMPROVISOR 2: Yeah, he messed that up.
INSTRUCTOR: No, he...
IMPROVISOR 2: Yeah, whatever. I like my idea better.

Got to be Real

In improv, there's a difference between inventing a new reality, and discovering what's happening in front of you and then responding with the next true and honest thing.

T.J. Jagadowski and David Pasquesi explain it this way in their incredible book, *Improvisation At The Speed of Life*:

"Discovery is realizing or uncovering what's already there. Its opposite is invention... Discovery is the path of least resistance, a state of non-doing and ease rather than force and effort. To us, invention (thinking up funny stuff) seems more difficult. It involves work, like an inventor toiling in a laboratory full of experiments. But discoverers? They can just stumble into the thing that's already there."

In other words, they add later, all we need to do is "pay attention to the show that is already carrying us down the river."

Back to the writing conference. It's after dinner, and there are now more than two dozen writers gathered together in the basement of the apartments at the college that plays host to what is simply referred to as St. Davids. Technically, it's campfire night, but rain has moved the event indoors. So while there's no fire, there are snacks and music, and my roommate Roberta, she of the nature walk, has been asked to tell a story.

Roberta is a drama teacher and she decides that, rather than tell the story herself, everyone should be involved in the fun. So she grabs an orange and explains to the group that she'll start the story and then pass the orange to someone else in the circle. They'll add a small bit to the tale and then pass the orange to someone else, and we'll go on like that until someone organically resolves the story.

It's another form of Yes, And.

Roberta starts by introducing us to a character named Jillian, who has just come home from work. As expected from a campfire story, it's a dark and stormy night, and as Jillian unlocks her front door and enters her house, she hears someone moving around upstairs. Which is weird, Roberta adds, because Jillian lives alone. And yet, as happens in all spooky stories, rather than calling 911, our heroine quietly makes her way up the stairs and down the dark hall to the spare bedroom.

Pass the orange.

The next few people add an open window, and billowing curtains, and wet footprints walking across the carpet despite the lack of another person in the room.

And then the orange comes to me.

I add that the bodyless footprints are now standing right in front of Jillian, and that the air blowing in from the open window carries the scent of lilac, the fragrance her dead grandmother always wore.

Pass the orange.

The story continues around the room. Someone adds a wedding dress in the closet; someone else tells us that the dress is normally stored in the attic but has mysteriously appeared in the spare bedroom. Another person informs us that Jillian's fiancé was killed in an accident; someone else reminds us of the bodyless footprints making their way across the carpet.

OK, I know what you're thinking....

GHOST!

We're almost back to the start of the circle as the orange passes to a woman who holds it for a moment before speaking. In the tense silence, we're all on the edge of our seats. We're almost done with the story, and we all know what should happen next.

"And then she woke up!" the woman cries, banging the orange down on the table.

An entire room full of writers groans. We all feel cheated out of the ending most of us were envisioning.

Later, over tea in our room, Roberta and I muse about why

the story never went where we all felt it was going: Jillian was being visited by her dead grandmother or her dead fiancé (or both!) on the eve of what would have been her wedding day. This was a room filled with writers, for heaven's sake. We know how to write a ghost story.

In hindsight, I admit that I, too, had dropped the ball. I could have just said that the footprints were being made by a dead grandmother. But I wanted to let someone else experience the "Aha!," that storytelling moment when the pieces all came together. So I added the scent of lilac and passed it off, expecting the next person to pick up on the hint. She didn't, and despite the hints that everyone dropped, no one made the bold move to say, "It's a ghost!"

I wonder aloud to Roberta. "Do you think that, because this is a Christian group, no one wanted to be the one to take the story in that direction?"

Probably not. We both laugh over the fact that when we played the game again—this time with Roberta and I actually acting out the story as people added to it—everyone eagerly put us in wild situations involving questionable parentage, bad dates, family turmoil, physical exercise (including tap dancing and jogging—thanks, guys), and a conclusion involving an incestuous relationship. So they definitely weren't shy about taking us to strange and weird places.

"I think it's just easier to tell the story when you actually see it unfolding in front of you," Roberta says, adding...

Got to be Real

"You forget about trying to think of something clever and just go with what's happening in the moment."

One of the improv lessons that has taken me the longest to learn is that if you're in a scene with bodyless, wet footprints and a dead grandmother, it's OK to just say, "It's a ghost!" I always felt doing that meant I was forcing my idea onto my scene partner.

But the truth is that dropping hints for your scene partner about what you think is happening, and hoping he'll say it for you, means you're expecting him to do the work.

And that's not being a supportive scene partner.

It also means that you assume that he is also thinking "Ghost!" when, in fact, he might be thinking "Dream sequence!" And when that happens, someone—most likely the audience—is going to be very disappointed.

So when everyone, including the audience, knows there's a ghost in the room, even if you don't actually believe in ghosts yourself, you need to just give the damned specter a name and put us all out of our creative agony.

If, however, there is not now and never has been a ghost in the scene, shouting "Ghost!" will not help the situation.

Got to be Real

Come on, people. You know when there's a ghost in the room.

Oh. And I should probably add this little improv advice as we close out this section...

Using a gun to shoot your partner and end the scene is the lazy way out of an awkward improv situation. It's better for the two of you to stick it out, support each other, and find the answer together.

But if someone does shoot you in a scene, take the bullet. We all know you were hit.

Better yet, don't be a lazy improvisor.
  Keep the improv gun in your pocket.

SMELLS LIKE TEAM SPIRIT

When explorers Lewis and Clark set out to find a way across the continent, they weren't creating places out of thin air as they trekked through the wilderness. They were discovering life as they found it, person by person, danger by danger, vista by vista, day by day.

They wanted to get from here to there and to see what was in between, so they journeyed out beyond the horizons, prepared as much as possible for the known but also open to the experiences they couldn't predict.

They weren't inventing. They were discovering.

And I imagine what they found was far more intricate and interesting and vast and beautiful than they could have imagined.

Think of yourself as an improvisational explorer, setting off in each scene to discover what lies beyond the horizon.

The pressure is off. You don't need to make anything up. You just need to be open to whatever might lie over the next mountain or what might wash up with the next wave. It could be poisonous snakes and enemies on horseback. But it also could be gorgeous sunsets and crystal streams.

Whatever it is, it'll probably be more exciting and more entertaining than whatever you had planned.

And never forget that you're not venturing out there alone.

Smells Like Team Spirit

SCENE FROM AN IMPROV SHOW: PART 1

We're standing on the stage, half of us on one side, half on the other, facing each other across the empty stage.

The show has begun, and there's a millisecond—just a fraction of a fraction of a fraction of a second—when nothing is happening, and no one has moved on the sidelines. It's just the blink of an eye, really, as we're all waiting to see what's going to happen.

We are feeling anxious.

There is no plan. There is no script. There is only the suggestion from the audience—it could be a word or a place; on this night it could be the zoo, a plunger, lipstick, a sewage treatment plant—and we're going to use that suggestion to inspire us to do something.

On stage.

In front of a live audience.

For a half hour.

There's a heartbeat...

Suddenly Stardust

...and then...

Smells Like Team Spirit

...one woman walks to the center of the stage and starts flapping her arms like a bird. The rest of us flock onto the stage and begin flapping, too.

We don't know where we are or why we're flapping our arms or if we're even birds.

But together, we're going to find out.

SCENE FROM AN IMPROV CLASS

IMPROVISORS stand in a circle. They've all been working on exercises and doing scenes together, and are preparing for a student showcase, the first of this second round of classes. The INSTRUCTOR for this level has been pushing the IMPROVISORS out of their comfort zones, working with them to do something that has no format, no structure, and no idea when it should begin or end, other than when it feels right.

There are no rules, and the answer to the question of "Should we..." is always "Yes." This causes a bit of anxiety because, in a few days, they're going to do it—whatever it is—in front an audience.

INSTRUCTOR: One at a time, you're going to voice to the group one thing that you're afraid of about improv. And then, one at a time, the rest of the team will reply with a sentence or two about how they're going to support you.

Everyone is silent for a moment, looking at each other, waiting for someone to start.

IMPROVISOR 1: I'll go. I'm afraid that when I get on stage, I won't know what to do or say.

Smells Like Team Spirit

One at a time, in random order, the other improvisors voice the ways they'll support their teammate.

IMPROVISOR 2: I'll support you by coming on stage with a strong initiation so you won't have to worry about making the first move.

IMPROVISOR 3: I'll support you by Yes, Anding everything you do or say.

IMPROVISOR 4: I'll support you by also not knowing what the hell we're doing on stage. I promise that you won't be out there alone.

IMPROVISOR 5: I'll support you by listening and by not getting anxious if there's silence, so that we can discover what's happening together.

IMPROVISOR 6: I'll support you by maintaining eye contact so you can give me a signal if you're feeling panicked, and we'll figure out how to move forward together.

And so on, until everyone has had a chance to speak.

By the time everyone has voiced a fear and had their teammates promise support, the IMPROVISORS have realized, maybe for the first time, how similar their own fears are to those of their teammates.

But now, they've pledged their support and also given themselves tools to stay connected during the show: making eye contact, actively listening, slowing down the pace, letting silence settle for a bit, speaking clearly, making bold choices.

Now, they know they are not alone.

Now, they are a team.

SCENE FROM AN IMPROV SHOW: PROLOGUE

Just before the show, as we are waiting in the wings for the host to introduce us, we turn to hug each other, look each other in the eye, and whisper, "I've got your back."

And we know it is true.

Smells Like Team Spirit

SCENE FROM AN IMPROV SHOW: PART 2

We're standing on stage, the team divided on the sidelines, facing each other across the empty stage.

We've been performing for 20 minutes and we can see the places, the people, the situations we've created all there in front of our eyes. We instinctively feel that the clock is ticking and it's time to try and bring the set full circle. Time has slowed. The fraction of a fraction of a fraction of a second now feels like minutes as we smile and make eye contact across the stage, some of us nodding a bit, some of us poised and ready to jump in however and whenever our teammates need us.

And then one person confidently steps forwards, his posture clearly communicating which character and which scene he's revisiting. Someone else steps out to join him. They interact. And then one of them offers up a gift, an opening for another team mate to join the scene, and then another, until organically we're all onstage in a group scene that ends our set.

The audience is laughing. We can hardly contain the high we're feeling.

Not because we are great performers.

Not because we are exceptionally talented.

Not because we've performed some wildly unique or inventive piece of theater.

But because we listened to each other and played together, and discovered the places and people and relationships that unfolded before our eyes as we thought of nothing except each moment as it came, each sentence as it was uttered, each small movement or voice inflection, focusing only on the person who was standing in front of us and our teammates on the sidelines.

Oh, there was an audience?

We hope they enjoyed the show. We sure did.

FEAR IS A FOUR-LETTER WORD

While I was writing this book, my publisher and I had several discussions about whether or not to spell out that "mother of all swear words" or use symbols and let you, the reader, fill in the blanks.

Words have power—and for many people, that one has nuclear power—and there's a fine line between using it for effect and being gratuitously crass. I hope by now you understand my intent was the former.

But hey, we're almost to the end of the book, and now I want to ask you something.

You know, just between us.

Fear is a Four-Letter Word

Which word do you believe has more power over your life?

☐ FUCK

☐ FEAR

By now you know that I spent a lifetime adhering to rules in order to live the life I was told I *should live*, existing primarily in fear of the repercussions of error and never once considering that the rules were keeping me from experiencing the life I *was meant to live*.

I was a mummy, wrapped in a shroud of worry, trapped in a tomb of my own making. And fear was my constant companion.

I used to think I was simply rationally questioning my own abilities whenever I stopped myself from pursuing something I wanted to do. You know, a little self doubt, just to keep myself honest with myself.

And in *The War of Art* author Steven Pressfield notes that a little self doubt *can* be a good thing, because it points us to our aspirations.

It's fear that stops us in our tracks.

SELF DOUBT /self-'daût/ *n.* lack of confidence in oneself and one's abilities.

FEAR /fir/ *n.* an unpleasant emotion caused by the belief that someone or something is dangerous, likely to cause pain, or a threat.

I've been musing for a while on the difference between self doubt and fear, and I think I finally understand it.

Fear is a Four-Letter Word

Self doubt asks, "Is this a good idea? Can you do it? I mean, really. Can *you* do *this*? Maybe. It won't be easy, and it's going to hurt. Are you sure you're up for this?"

This is when we need to Yes, And ourselves, keeping our eye on our heart's desire. Sure, we might take three steps ahead and two steps back, but the key is that even if we're falling, we're falling forward.

Fear? That's our inner critic on steroids, and it's so powerful that it only needs to croon softly in our ear to make its point. "You? *You?* My, my, my. Don't we think highly of ourselves? You're out of your league, baby. You know, this could kill you. Do you really want to take that chance?"

Fear wants to keep us frozen in place, because it knows that if we act, the insidious little monster will diminish bit by bit until it's relegated to the back lines.

Fear is a Four-Letter Word

And fear doesn't play second fiddle to anyone.
    It'll burn the house down before it loses the upper hand.

This is when we need to stand our ground, look fear in the face, and then fight right through it, into the fire, through the flames, trudging through the coals, knowing that every bold move that follows will leave battle scars.

But we'll be more beautiful for it.

Fear is a Four-Letter Word

Everything worth pursuing in life comes with pain—growth itself is literally painful (that's why they're called growing pains).

And yes, sometimes growth is dangerous. Not every caterpillar survives the transformation to butterfly.

And yet growth is vital to life, to beauty, to community. Everything that advances the causes of justice is a threat to the status quo, yet without action your fellow man suffers. Fear's goal is to stop progress, thwart justice, stomp on beauty. It doesn't need an army. Fear just needs someone willing to listen to its whisper.

Suddenly Stardust

So let the self doubt act as your aspirational compass.
  But kick fear in the teeth and move forward, one step at a time.

Fear is a Four-Letter Word

You've got business to attend to, Buttercup.
  The world is waiting.

Suddenly Stardust

Dennis is standing down stage right. He's playing the character of a hard boiled detective and I am his ditzy secretary, complete with the squeaky, high pitched voice. I stand just about center stage. Dennis is facing me; he's just spoken and is awaiting my reply.

I have only known Dennis for a few weeks. We're currently halfway through a season of a long form performance league, where improvisors sign up for twelve week sessions and are randomly put into teams. Each team is given a coach; teams meet weekly for practice and bi-weekly for shows. At the end of twelve weeks, teams and coaches are shuffled and a new season begins.

The goal is for improvisors of all experience levels to get together to hone their skills, have fun, and foster community spirit.

Our coach has decided that for this session we'll work on a format called "the movie", meaning that for each bi-weekly performance we improvise a 20-minute movie in a genre suggested by the audience. There is no script; this movie is completely improvised.

And it's scary.

Dennis is one of the kindest people I've met so far in this league, which I joined on a whim hoping to get to know other improvisors and maybe find a new team after the theater where I'd been doing short form improv closed. Despite the fact that he's young enough to be my son, Dennis and I have enjoyed playing together. Maybe it's because he's sensitive to the fact that I'm still feeling my way around this movie format, as well as long form improv in general. I trust him when we get onstage.

On this night the audience has given us the genre of film noir, and over the last fifteen minutes our team has created an intricate movie plot line involving a possible alien invasion, doubting government officials, and reports that a UFO may have crashed in an apple orchard outside of our city. We began our set in an office, where Dennis and I stepped into roles of detective and secretary who have unearthed a government coverup, and the story has eventually led us to the climax of our set, here, to the apple orchard, where we are going to investigate the alien wreckage.

We are overjoyed at the discovery. It's then that Dennis, as detective, turns to me and asks excitedly:

DENNIS: Do you know what this means?

I hold my breath as I lock eyes with Dennis. In one sense, he's just violated an (alleged) cardinal rule of improv. He asked me a question that leaves me with the responsibility to figure out what's happening.

For a heartbeat, I fear my inexperience will screw up the set that, so far, has been moving along swimmingly. I don't want to make a mistake by misreading anything. I don't want to sabotage the momentum our team has built together by inadvertently moving us in the wrong direction.

This is a lot of pressure. For a single heartbeat, I doubt myself.

But then my heart beats again and puts the panic at bay. I understand that my scene partner has not thrown me under a bus with this question. Quite the opposite, in fact. This question is the most natural thing in the world for a detective to ask his faithful sidekick at this point in their journey.

And in this moment, that's exactly who we are. He is the boss, I am his secretary. Of course I will take a moment to consider his question and then, in wide-eyed wonder, take in everything in front of me before answering.

I view this world our team has created with such intricate detail.

I *am* standing in an apple orchard. There is a UFO, down stage right, crashed among the apple trees. There is smoldering wreckage everywhere. I don't need to invent anything. I can see the twisted, otherworldly metal, smell the smoke from burning alien fuel, hear the hiss and pop of fruit as it explodes from the heat, see the hole in the ground where the prized crops once stood.

What does this mean? he's asked. The audience is waiting to hear my answer, too. I nod slowly and reply in my character's squeaky voice, tentatively at first, my excitement growing with each syllable, as if the answer is dawning on me as the words are coming out of my mouth.

Because that's exactly what's happening.

ME *(turning slowly to look Dennis in the eye)*: The... apple harvest...is... going to be... late this year!

I don't realize until much later that the audience roars when I deliver that line, which came from left field, even to me. I only know that Dennis and I are smiling at each other, because yes, that was exactly the right response, even if we didn't know it until the words left my lips.

Recalling it now, I'm not even sure why it was funny, although I laugh every time I think about it. All I know is that Dennis and I were on the same page, and the audience was with us.

I didn't have to worry about what I was going to say. I only had to live in the world our team had created, to listen, to do the next honest thing my character would do.

I only had to open my mouth and set free whatever words were waiting to fall from my lips.

THINGS I HAVE SAID YES, AND TO SINCE I STARTED DOING IMPROV:

Having friends.
Playing.
Laughing.
Laughing maniacally.
Dancing.
Dancing in public.
Going out after dark.
Speaking my mind.
Listening.
Finding ways to agree with people I disagree with.
Accepting things as they are instead of how I wish they were.
Asking for things I need.
Spending time alone.
Saying no to toxic people and situations.
Learning to manage in seemingly unmanageable situations.
Making mistakes.
Trying and failing.
Trying and succeeding.

Fear is a Four-Letter Word

THINGS I STILL DO:

Doubt myself.
Ask questions.
Apologize.
Cry.

Improv didn't change everything about me.
   Nor should it.

Fear is a Four-Letter Word

I am who I am.
   You are who you are.

We are what we create, as we inhale and exhale stardust. Together.

End of scene.

ACKNOWLEDGMENTS & NOTES

I've been deeply blessed to have had the opportunity to learn from incredibly talented instructors and to have the support of some of the kindest and most talented humans on earth. I wish I could list every single one of you but there's not enough room. To those of you who taught me, listened to me cry, pushed me outside of my comfort zone, read early versions of this book, and generally loved me through my creative transitions—a heartfelt thank you. OK, a few of you do need a special shout out:

Village Idiots Improv; Rochester Long Form League; The Urge; Awkwards Anonymous; Living Room Sessions; Easily Amused; St. Davids Writers' Conference; Robin Schiffrin; Laura Normandy; Laura Fleming; Stephanie Barnes; Scott Baker; Austin Scott; Nick Rabb; Megan Mack; Jeff Andrews; Wendy Liebman; Carrie Anne Noble; Roberta Gore; Amy Mable; Linda Au; Crystal Hayduk; Sara Moore; Linsay Bell.

Thank you to Law Tarello, who first told me to fuck the rules—and then shoved me out of my creative cage.

To be a performer without a place to perform is a small form of creative torture. Thank you to Focus Theater's John Forrest Thompson, Roger Sutphen, Tim Shea, and Keith Gomez for providing a loving, supportive physical home to Rochester's improv community.

WordCraft's Mike and Paula Parker are more than just publishers, writers, and creative inspirations. They are dear

Acknowledgments & Notes

friends. Thank you for giving life to the quirky book that spilled out of my heart. (And thank you for leaving the swearing in there; I hope the message was worth the risk.)

Thank you to my father Jim, my mother Judy, and my sister Jackie for laughing at my jokes and encouraging me my entire life, even if you weren't always exactly sure what I was doing.

Thank you, Cassie, for being an entertaining, loving, and creative daughter, and for always telling me I have pretty hair. (Shall I perform *Death of a Butterfly* for you?)

And most importantly, thank you to darling husband Dave, for allowing me to pursue this weird creative life while you hold down a real job. I am grateful beyond words for... well, everything. I love you.

NOTES

"Flecks of Extraterrestrial Dust, All Over the Roof"
by William J. Broad
The New York Times, March 10, 2017

"Disrupting the flow: How brief silences in group conversations affect social needs,"
by Koudenburg, N., et al.
Journal of Experimental Social Psychology (2011)

Improvisation at the Speed of Life
by David Pasquesi and T. J. Jagodowski
Solo Roma, Inc

The War of Art: Break Through the Blocks and Win Your Inner Creative Battles
by Steven Pressfield
Black Irish Entertainment LLC

Self-Doubt and Fear
definitions by Merriam Webster Dictionary

Acknowledgments & Notes

ABOUT THE AUTHOR

Improvisor, author, actor, and award-winning writer Joanne Brokaw performs regularly at The Focus Theater as part of the house team The Urge. She is also a member of the comedy trio Easily Amused and the improv duo A Happy Accident.

Joanne lives in Rochester, New York, where she writes, performs, and leads improv workshops to help people push past fear, embrace creativity, and learn to play again.

Learn more about her at:
www.joannebrokaw.com

ALSO AVAILABLE FROM
WORDCRAFTS PRESS

Aerobics for the Mind
  by Michael Potts, PhD

Elders at the Gate
  by Ray Blunt

Shameless Self Promotion
  by Paula K. Parker, Mike Parker, & Torry Martin

Geezer Stories: The Care & Feeding of Old People
  by Laura Mansfield

Embracing a New Vision of Aging
  By Sheryl Towers

www.WordCrafts.net

www.ingramcontent.com/pod-product-compliance
Lightning Source LLC
Chambersburg PA
CBHW030055100526
44591CB00008B/156